Unmasked

A Child and Adolescent Psychiatrist's Memoir of the COVID-19 Pandemic

Dr N.J. Nadeem

Acknowledgements

Dedicated to my beloved husband, children, family, friends, inspiring colleagues and mentors. Thank you for supporting me during my 'unmasked moments'. You are my anchors in the stormy sea of life. You are my uplifting wings. I value your ongoing guidance, motivation and encouragement. It's been a true team effort! My heartfelt prayers to you all…

About the author

Dr N.J. Nadeem
MRCPsych MBBS MA DCH BMedSci

Dr N.J. Nadeem holds impressive academic qualifications including being a Member of the Royal College of Psychiatrists (UK), Masters in International Child Studies, Diploma in Child Health, Bachelors in Medicine and Community Health Sciences.

Dr N.J. Nadeem is a Child and Adolescent Psychiatrist trained and based in London, United Kingdom with an outstanding track record in clinical practice, teaching and research. Dr N.J. Nadeem has significantly contributed to the medical field by authoring numerous publications in esteemed medical journals and other media including magazine/newspapers. She regularly attends and speaks at national and international conferences where she shares her work and valuable experience.

As an Honorary Clinical Lecturer and Faculty Member on a Postgraduate Child Psychiatry course, Dr N.J. Nadeem is deeply committed to education. She engages in teaching sessions and has conducted workshops for medical students, junior doctors, and other healthcare professionals globally.

Prologue

This is a memoir of my experiences in the first 21 days on the journey up to the COVID-19 pandemic peak with reflections and insights on boosting psychological immunity and coping in unprecedented times of uncertainty and crisis. I hope many others may benefit from my words and advice and those who know me will feel as though I am talking directly to them. For those who do not know me, I hope you find my words soothing, and if I can help even one person climb out of a difficult place and improve their life, I will have achieved my mission. I hope I have put into writing the words you need to hear. Maybe you do not need to hear them today, but one day, I hope and pray that in my words you find peace, solace, joy and satisfaction.

Day 1 – 17 March 2020

The year 2020 will go down in history just as many other major worldwide events, tragedies and atrocities have done before. To mention just a few: world wars, 9/11 and the 2004 Boxing day tsunami. 2020 is the year the world closed for business; not just neighbourhoods, not just cities but whole countries have effectively closed down. Major financial hubs, international transit zones, global sporting tournaments and many other international events have been cancelled/closed, countries have shut their borders and sealed their citizens inside. Life is on hold for now for countless millions around the world and not a single person in the world can even give a good estimate of when normality as we once knew it will return.

We all have high hopes for our future and the future of our children. However, at the moment, everything seems tragically bleak. There seems to be no way out of this. There is no escape. If only we could travel to a deserted island somewhere far, far away from everyone else just to be safe. The fear of this deadly virus is far beyond what most of us will have ever even imagined. Yes, we may have seen various sci-fi movies about such things, but these scenarios and events only ever happen in the movies, right? Not anymore it seems. It feels as though we are living in a movie now. If only it were just an awful dream, a dreadful nightmare unfolding before us. There is absolutely no way out of this terrible nightmare. We have to ride the storm and see it through until the end, hoping that there is an end which seems a distant dream. As of today, there does not appear to be a light at the end of this extremely dark, silent and never-ending tunnel. Not to mention, lonely. With millions of people self-isolating or in quarantine, cutting themselves off from the outer world, a new way of life is emerging. This is not how life should be. This is not how life has ever been for us. This is not life as we know it.

'Self-isolation, social distancing, flattening the curve'; terminologies most of us have never even heard of. Now, we hear these words and phrases more than any others. Common language nowadays. It feels as though there is nothing else to talk about, nothing else to focus on. It is the main topic in any social circle, any meeting, any conversation. All energies are being focused on COVID-19 and how to improve our chances of getting out of this predicament alive.

A major aspect of humanity is our interaction and relationship with other people and with our environment. We are by our innate nature essentially social animals. We need each other, and how can we even begin to contemplate a life without each other? By now many people (not just in the UK but globally) have understood and accepted the unbearable fact that we are all a risk to each other, and the only way to protect ourselves and others is to stay away from each other. Heartbreaking as it is, if we stay away from our loved ones now, only then we can hope and pray to meet again. This is termed 'social distancing' and is a term used flippantly all of the time now. What people really mean to say is 'physical distancing'. The social side of things we need now more than ever before! We need to reach out to each other, help and support each other, be a shoulder to cry on. Of course, not literally but in a physically distant manner! From this physical distance we must keep in touch, connect and engage with our loved ones.

It's just the beginning of who knows what…

Day 2 – 18 March 2020

Today we begin our first day in social isolation as both of our toddlers developed a high fever overnight. We have had a rough night and we wake to wonder how we will cope and what little the little ones know about what is going on in the world! Such an unprecedented historical time which will probably shape their future to a great extent, and they will most probably have very little memory of it, or no memory of it at all. Perhaps an even scarier thought…what if the current times becomes their first and earliest memory? No one would want that for their children. Everyone wishes their children to have happy memories of enjoying themselves outdoors in a relaxed environment surrounded by their friends and families. Surrounded by other children, playing the park on sunny days, walking in the rain with their little cartoon-printed umbrellas and wellington boots, splashing in the puddles as they toddle by. This all seems like a distant dream as we realise the inevitable reality now.

It feels like we are cut-off from everyone else, disconnected from our friends and family. Now even our loved ones who live around the corner feel as though they are just as far away as our loved ones who live thousands of miles away in other countries. Thank God for technology! At the very least we can call/video each other for as long as we want, all for free too; at least somethings are unrestricted and have not been cancelled/closed! It's not all doom and gloom. We are only maintaining a physical distance and we are otherwise keeping in constant touch with others by social media and calls; albeit there is only one topic of conversation on any forum! So many videos, so many updates and articles. Information overload beware! Perhaps it is this very technology that will keep us sane, perhaps it will have the opposite effect.

Only time will tell…

Day 3 – 19 March 2020

Yesterday it was announced that schools will close…except for children of keyworkers. Telling my children this news was fun! They have been waiting with eager anticipation for this news; after all, we all knew it was coming. From the children's perspective they perhaps saw it as one long holiday; maybe in their naivety they do not realise what this means. Staying at home for a prolonged period of time, not seeing any friends, no family, no outings, nothing. What little do they know that the safest place for them is at home.

When they heard the news, they were literally ecstatic and jumping with joy. Squealing away amongst themselves, they struggled to contain themselves. It was a real pleasure to watch their happiness at schools being closed until further notice. That is until we gave them the next piece of information that applied specifically to them. Schools are to remain open for children of keyworkers including doctors. Upon hearing this, their elated smiles were immediately wiped off their cute little faces. This is unbelievable and grossly unjust according to them. The look in their eyes was truly awful, as if to say, *Why do I have a mum who is a doctor?* Usually, they beam with pride at this fact and proudly announce it to their friends in the playgrounds. They are always the first to put their hands up in class to share with the other kids about their families etc. Today was different. The look of regret and dismay as though they are being punished because their mum is a doctor.

We removed them from their misery almost instantaneously as we could not bear to see their distress. We told them that yes this is the guidance but if children have one parent who is able to work from home, then they can stay at home too. No school for them then, and they are relieved that at least one of their parents is not a keyworker! The regretful looks on their faces of how unfortunate they felt to have a parent as a doctor was unbearable. They should feel proud to have parents in such roles.

Once again, they yo-yo back up and their elation escalates to levels they cannot contain. Beaming and bouncing around, it's smiles all round. A mini party erupted in our living room as they eagerly anticipated a vacation. As parents, we just want to bubble wrap them as much as we possibly can and keep them away from any risk of exposure. Who knows when schools will reopen? Are we talking weeks or months? No one knows. For now we are simply enjoying the feeling of 'schools out' with our children.

Day 4 – 20 March 2020

Yet more measures announced today…all entertainment venues to close until further notice. All to avoid people coming into close contact with one another. We must avoid visiting elderly/vulnerable people, regardless of relation. We must cocoon them from others; there is no other way. This virus sees no relation, it observes no barriers. Even if they are your closest nearest and dearest, we must not come into close contact with them, unless we live in the same household. What sort of dire situation is this?

It feels as though the world, its infrastructure, even its people, are steadily, gradually and rapidly closing down. How will we get through this? How will we recover? It just goes to show that things that we base our lives around – cafes, restaurants, gyms, cinemas etc. – are all secondary as though they are the sprinkles on top of a cupcake. They are the extras we can live without, if we really have to. What we can't live without, and can't even bear contemplating living without, is each other.

In some ways it is all about priorities now. The priorities are crystal clear: health, family and food. Everything else can and will be compromised on. We need to hunker down in the comfort of our own homes and ride out the storm. We know it is coming, but we have no idea how bad it will be, and we don't even know who will remain on the other side. Such depressing thoughts, but this is the current reality. For the first time in our living memory, if not in recent history, all we have to do collectively and simultaneously is stay at home to save lives. Essentially, stay at home so we can stay away from other people. This is what needs to be done if we want to survive this storm. It seems so simple, and, in some ways, it is, but in other ways and for some people it may not be that straight forward.

We need to forget our old ways, ignore cultural attitudes and norms. Life right now is not normal; it is in fact far from normal. These are not normal times. We are facing an invisible enemy of immense magnitude, and the frustrating thing is that we cannot blame anyone. Who can we point fingers at? In all previous historical mass scale atrocities, we have always had someone to blame: an individual, a group, a country etc. Something tangible is usually there for us to direct our anger towards, e.g. WW1, WW2, 9/11 etc. We often externalise our anger and project blame somewhere. In this current climate, we do not have a definite tangible entity to blame. This enemy respects no one; no races, no religions, no social classes are safe from it. It defies all boundaries. It has no doubt brought us to our knees and we are all now on one level footing. It will wipe out the best of us; it will spare no one. Our fragility and vulnerability are evident now; just rewind your life back to only a few weeks ago and you will understand this. What was your daily routine? What were the societal norms? And where are we today? Where will we be in a few weeks' time? A few months' time?

The capacity of the human spirit to adapt is truly astounding. Norms and measures which under normal circumstances would cause so much upheaval and backlash are being accepted and implemented by the vast majority of people. The minority that are not following the new rules, what can we say about them? Do they not comprehend? Is it ignorance, naivety or something else? Do they feel all powerful against this enemy? Are they being unethical or immoral? All controversial statements. When news of this virus first came out, the general feeling was that this is happening elsewhere, far, far away on distant shores. Sure, it's devastating, but it's not happening here. We are safe. How things can change so fast, faster than we can imagine. We are now in the midst of it. Even then, a small minority of people are continuing with their previous norms. We need to forget past ways, adopt this new way of life; it is the only way to pull through it.

Until and unless people feel that they or their loved one is at risk, they will not change their ways. They will remain in denial; they will ignore advice. They will continue to mix and mingle with the very people they want to protect. In this war, the doctors and other healthcare staff are the soldiers. We are the defence. The enemy is firing at us from all angles and has made humans its carriers. Invisible firing from invisible carriers who are innocently and naively supporting the enemy. This is innocent betrayal and will kill so many of us. Then who will we blame? We will blame ourselves for not keeping away from other people. How will we live with that guilt? This is a generation-defining moment and everything we do now will go down in history... the generation that stayed away from each other to keep each other alive.

Day 5 – 21 March 2020

A new dawn, a new beginning; the sun has risen as it always does and for a split second, still half asleep and dozy, I have forgotten about the current crisis. It's nice to have forgotten about it for a moment and important too to re-energise ourselves to face the future. Reality hits home; we are self-isolating at home two preteens who constantly pick up over nothing and two sick toddlers. We spend our days and nights monitoring their temperatures and wrestling with them to get some paracetamol in them. They appear brighter today, and their temperatures are lower.

It feels that we are on a deserted island all alone. We have bubble wrapped our family to protect ourselves, as well as to protect other people. It's still early days in this 14-day self-isolation period and even after this we will continue to stay at home unless absolutely necessary. We are taking it seriously and wish that other people would too. It won't be forever like this, we hope, but definitely for the foreseeable future. Until very recently we had been making future plans like we always do: holiday plans, outing plans, activities we want to do, restaurants we want to go to. All of this is now on hold. We don't even think about making any plans. The only plan now is survival. Any plans we make now are linked to this: what should we be doing? What can we do better?We have forgotten our former way of life. The sooner we all adopt the new way of life, the better. Of course, once I am out of this 14-day period I will return to work at the hospital, not because I have to but because I want to, I need to. I can't say at home if I could be out there helping others in these most difficult times. We are the soldiers in this war and some of us will die in service as many soldiers have died in previous wars. This time it will be no different. I hope my family can remain at home for as long as possible and minimise their exposure. I will be piercing through the bubble wrap every time I go to the hospital to help.

The future prospects appear daunting. We cannot even begin to imagine what tsunami is fast approaching us. Soon people will be dropping dead like flies, bodies will be stacking up and mortuaries will overflow. Even funerals will become a luxury. People will be afraid of attending and burying their loved ones. It will be a lonely death for many people and an even lonelier grieving process for those left behind. Psychological trauma and distress will become the new norm. We are not the first humans to face such atrocities; it has happened many times before now. It is simply our turn.

For now, we don't know how long we are in this for. Is it a short sprint or will this be the longest marathon ever? A haunting uncertainty awaits us as we edge closer and closer each day. There is no escape. There is no way out. There isn't even a shortcut! Until a few weeks ago, we lived in a time where everything was possible; we felt invincible, thanks to developments in technology and scientific progress.

Today, the world is on its knees, hopeless, fearful and dreading what is coming next… Will this dark grey cloud have a silver lining at all? Unlikely for those who lose an important loved one.

Life will never be the same again…

Day 6 – 22 March 2020

The UK has now an excess of 5000 positive cases. This is the news we wake up to; how very demoralising and depressing. The predictions are that this number will continue to increase at an ever-alarming rate. Just as we absorb and digest one set of figures, a new dawn brings with it another set of numbers for us to spend the day pondering and contemplating. It is as though we are stuck in a vicious cycle with a vicious trajectory. Across the world the figures are escalating at such an alarming rate, it is it is difficult to keep up with it. Many countries have implemented stricter measures than the UK including closing borders, stay at home measures and complete lockdown of cities. Here, measures are comparatively less ruthless; massively inconvenient, yes, but not yet ruthless or draconian (a buzzword nowadays). We hope that the British people are heeding Public Health England's advice of social distancing and isolation. It is clear that many are trying their best; it is also evident that many are not. Pleasure and entertainment complexes are closed but now people are gathering in parks, beaches and if nothing else there are queues and crowds around grocery stores. This is doing nothing to contain the virus. People are continuing to spread it. It is not spreading by itself. The people are the problem, and the people are the solution. We are capable of both carrying and assisting the enemy as well as being the line of defence; which side are you taking? The concepts of social distancing and isolation form the backbone of the defence in this war. Although it has changed the very fabric of society, do we have any other option? Is there any way out of this? Each day now is valuable, and speed is of the essence. We must change our actions and behaviours. We should have changed our way sooner, instead of watching and waiting complacently. We must bow our heads, forget all norms, kill our egos in order to save ourselves as well as others. Humanity is at stake. Everything is being cancelled, closed, shut down, and for some, life will also be shut down.

On a positive note, today is Mother's Day celebratedtraditionally by people buyinggifts for their mothers and spend the day with them to show their love and appreciation. Today for the first time ever, people are showing their love and appreciation by staying away physically. The maximum that people are doing is delivering their gifts at their mum's doorstep and waving from across the road. All to keep their mum safe. Tragic times. This is the new reality. If you want someone to survive this, stay away from them. It is the oddest predicament and seems to contradict and oppose our gut instincts. Now we have to stay away from those we love otherwise they might die. Then what's the point? We would rather stay away than the alternative.

Today is our fifth day of social isolation. The toddlers are now feeling much better and are recovering well from whatever bug they had. We dread to think it may have been COVID-19 but they are better now and that's the main thing. We know this current crisis is going to go on for the next few months at least. In fact, it has only just begun. We are only at the foot of the hill and as we regularly look up, we can imagine and foresee where we are going. The wipeout of human beings is coming. Many will survive, many will not. For many, their deadline is approaching fast. Literally.

As we know we will be at home for some time, today we have begun to think about how we will manage. We need to think about food supplies, activities for children, education for them etc. One approach we are considering is to try to follow the school timetable, so the kids have a structured routine of study time, mealtimes, break times, bath and bedtime. Maintaining a routine is vital at any time as well as during a crisis. It allows us to get on with things, sometimes in autopilot mode when we don't feel like it. It also acts as an anchor grounding us in times of anxiety. So, I have decided for my family to set aims for the day and plan one activity per day. This way we have something to look forward to and hopefully it will help us to maintain some level of normality in what is otherwise a wildly abnormal situation.

Let's see how it goes…

Day 7 – 23 March 2020

Yesterday evening, unsurprisingly there were another 700 or so cases and 40 or so more deaths in the UK. Now this isn't coming as a shock; we have accepted this as another aspect of this new norm. At night, while we restfully sleep, we know that more people will die. We know we will awake to more tragic news, and a feeling of acceptance has begun. The initial feeling of shock, horror, denial and dread are now transforming into feelings of mourning and remorse. At some times, the feeling of dread. At some point, we will start hearing of the deaths of a 'friend of a friend' or acquaintances, colleagues, friends, the shopkeeper, the guy who lives on such and such road, and even loved ones.

The government has been doing their daily press briefings and yesterday was no exception. But today's was somewhat different to the previous few. It left a positive vibe. Don't get me wrong; in previous press briefings the government has been positive, hopeful and honest. Today's was different; it was truly heartwarming and compassionate. It left a feeling of pride, proud to be a citizen of the UK, proud of the British values. It's truly amazing what can be achieved if we all pull together as a united team and have only one enemy. We are all in this together and each and every one of us has an important role to play. In such a short space of time, the government has arranged an intensive support package for the 1.5 million people in the UK who have the most serious underlying health conditions. Identifying and highlighting these vulnerable people and providing food and medicine services to their door is no easy task, and what a fast turnaround. It's truly commendable. Hundreds and thousands of people have signed up to volunteer to help those who are unable to manage on their own. So many acts of kindness, so many innovative ideas. For example, putting up pictures that kids are drawing so people who are walking past can look at them, singing from balconies etc. It's heartwarming to see humanity at its best and has done a great job of instilling positivity and hope in a time where everything seems so drastically negative and it's hard to muster the courage and hope needed to climb this unsurmountable mountain. People think climbing Mount Everest is tough; try imagining the climb we are facing. At the moment, we are still comfortably at the foot of the mountain on a comparative basis to where we will soon be. There has been much controversy recently on the news and backlash at the UK government's strategy and management of this crisis, but today's 'shielding' concept is truly compassionate. Almost every other day we are being introduced to a new concept. Today was 'shielding'.

In the recent days, things have changed at a drastic speed like never before. We have had to adapt fast. There is no time to think and ponder and there is even very little time to discuss and debate. Things that in previously normal times would take weeks, months or even years to get approval and implementation are being turned over and out at an unbelievable speed. Impressive, it seems, but we have no other option but to step up our approach. The capacity of the human mind to adapt and cope is truly astonishing. We suddenly find that we have psychological reserves we knew nothing about. We are having to dig deep into our backup psychological mental health systems to get through the day. Now we live one day at a time. At the moment, it is difficult to imagine a life without COVID-19. As if we have been transported to a parallel universe.

Is this really happening? Is it all a very dreadful nightmare?

Day 8 – 24 March 2020

Everyone is carrying the virus until proven otherwise. Such facts are terrifying and enough to give anyone goosebumps. It makes us shiver, just contemplating that this could very easily be true, if not now then very soon. I am now beginning to realise that pretty much all I have written about so far is so negative, dreadful and demoralising. Even if the current reality is like this, we must still focus on something positive. There is no time like the present to take extra care of our mental health, to build up our psychological research and boost our morale. We may not feel like doing anything and COVID-19 fever has taken over the planet as well as our headspace. As though we have no space left in our minds to focus on anything else. Is there even anything else to focus on at the moment except how to protect our families from the virus? That's how it feels but this is not how it needs to be. Start today and jumpstart yourself back to good mental health!

No one will be the same on the other side of this mountain. Some of us will not be fortunate enough to be here anymore. We need to kickstart our mental health which for most people (regardless of whether they have underlying mental health issues or not) has deteriorated recently, all thanks to the virus. We need to not only take physical precautions (PPE, social distancing etc). We must also simultaneously take psychological precautions so that we are in a better position to face the upcoming tragic phase in our lives. Where should we start? There are so many avenues and strategies we can and should be working on to build our reserves. Let's start with one of the basic simplest concepts of social support. Now more than ever before we need to (metaphorically!) hold hands and pull each other closer towards us. We need to reach out to others, be a listening ear, a shoulder to cry on. We need to form a chain of support around us.

We have heard the buzzword 'chains' so much recently in various contexts; for example, chains of transmission and supply chains. What we need now are social chains so we can ringfence our psychological well-being and pre-empt any deterioration. We are all in this together in the same boat, ready and braced to ride the gigantic waves. At times we will fall under, at times we will feel as though we are drowning, but we will rise up, and at some point, there will be smooth sailing again.

In the meantime, and from now, we should strengthen our relationships. Forgive and forget past grievances and reconnect with those with whom the connection has weakened. We cannot carry any extra baggage on this boat; if we all continue to carry our emotional baggage and step onto this boat, the boat will sink under the weight of the collective baggage. It won't need the upcoming surge of COVID-19 to tip us overboard and submerge our boat. Undoubtedly, it's an immensely difficult task to throw overboard our issues and past hurts, but even if we are able to get rid of some of these it will lighten our load. In many cases, it may not be possible to completely wipe the slate clean and start from afresh. It would be an ideal approach, but not necessarily realistic. Emotions and feelings are like that; deep, complex and convoluted in their very nature. We should simply try our best. Whatever emotional pain you are able to lock away in a folder, place the folder inside the treasure box and throw it into the vast ocean. I urge you to do this. Lighten your load, relieve yourself from the weights you carry. Let go of the emotions connected to events from the past. No one is saying that you should forget your past struggles, of course not. Those painful struggles have made you the person you are today. All you need to do is decrease the emotional burden associated with these negative memories. This would be the first step to improving our social chains and personal relationships. How much emotional weight are you carrying? What is the point? Surely, it is better to free yourself, your heart and your mind. Give yourself the permission to free yourself of the hurt caused by others. These shackles are damaging you more than anyone else. Definitely learn from those incidents and carry this with you. Just realise the emotions attached to it, file it away in a secure folder, lock it in the treasure chest and chuck it into the ocean. Often words alone do not help, and this is where the power of visual imagery can be used. Take the time to really try to picture in your mind. Close your eyes and visualise yourself taking these steps. See yourself open and closing the file once and for all. Notice the details of the file, the colour and the texture. Imagine the clunking sound of the key, the lid banging closed, and hear the sound of it crashing into the ocean. Imagine feeling light and relaxed as you no longer carry the cumbersome weight. Feel free!

Some emotional weight is harder to file away and dispose of, but you must try. Only for yourself. You deserve better than to carry your weights given to you by other people. Those issues that you're struggling to process and file away, don't punish yourself for not being able to disconnect from them. At least you are trying, and you should applaud yourself for trying. You will never be completely weight-free, for you are human, after all, not a robot or a computer system that can be wiped clean or rebooted! Your aim is to minimise your emotional baggage as much as possible. That's all.

The word 'control' is also being bounded around in the news nowadays and it is a very interesting one. As a democratic society, we are generally independent and in control of our lives. Discussions now are about the government imposing measures to control our behaviour and movements in an attempt to curb the spread of the virus. That is 'lockdown', another buzzword nowadays. We know lockdown is coming in the UK, it is just a matter of time. When this happens, we will lose our independence and freedom as well as our sense of control over our lives. What can we do to improve this feeling? This sense of control is another interesting concept, and the key thing is to recognise and acknowledge that some things in life are beyond our control. We must allow ourselves to let go of things that we cannot control. Accept this. For example, we cannot control the spread of this virus, the actions of other people in social distancing and isolating. Take control of what we can...the small things etc.

What a fine day we wake up to… only in terms of the weather though. Everything else in life is far from fine. There is an eerie silence outside, and no movement can be seen from our window. As though everyone and everything has ceased to exist. A stark contrast to the usual hustle and bustle early on Tuesday morning. We are used to hearing the sounds of people banging the front door closed, shouts of 'Bye, see you later', cars whizzing down the road, and most hilariously, parents screaming at their kids, 'Hurry up, get ready, it's getting late for school!' When will these fond busy chaotic days return? Not any time soon; today is only day one of lockdown!

Serene and still outside, yet anxious and apprehensive inside. The war is raging; all we are getting now is the mild gurgles. The volcano will soon erupt, spewing its moltenous lava across the nation. Its ripples will affect us for years to come, for generations to come.

Lockdown or locked up? For millions of people across the globe, the country has been locked down, but on a personal level it feels like we have been locked up in our own homes. Some of us have the liberty to leave our premises but only if we have good enough, valid reasons. Only those who are playing an important role in the fight against COVID-19 have the luxury of being allowed to step foot into the outer world. Though is this a luxury for them? They too are at risk, and they too have families and personal commitments. They risk their lives and are putting their lives on the line to go out there to quite literally confront COVID-19, look at it in the face directly and fight it. Do these doctors, nurses and many others not feel fear? Are they truly courageous? Are they heroes? No, none of these. They are merely immensely humane individuals who cannot simply give up and stay at home, knowing that they have the skills, training and expertise to help someone. Not just help but save a life. Saving families from being torn apart by COVID-19. Of course, they feel fear just as much as anyone else must be feeling… if not more given that they are directly confronting the invisible killer head on. But when you see them on the front line in the hospitals, they will not look afraid. They will not allow it to show on their faces. They will maintain their composure and put their personal anxieties to one side. They are there to look after you, safeguard your life and save as many lives as possible. These doctors will reassure you, give you hope and will do their very best to instil calm and positivity in otherwise the bleakest of times. But who will safeguard them? Who will look after them?

We have to look after each other both physically and mentally...

Day 9 – 25 March 2020

Today I feel physically sick, with symptoms of nausea and chest heaviness, as though I can't breathe easily, and I'm psychologically anxious and fearful. Yesterday the UK's deaths increased by 87. This is the first largest jump. These symptoms of anxiety, fear and dread come and go usually after reading the latest figures. Like many people across the globe, I have been closely following the latest developments in the war against the virus. Initially, it was interesting, informative and important in keeping up to date. At that point, it felt distant, happening elsewhere to others in the world far, far away. Over the past few weeks, the feeling has changed. The reality has also changed. This is now feeling very much more personal. It is now not only on home soil, but it also feels as though it is in my backyard, knocking on my front door, knocking on my windows. I know that these symptoms are of anxiety. Of course I have studied it, seen it and treated many patients with anxiety over the years.

In the current climate of the COVID-19 pandemic, anxiety and fear is understandable. It is normal to feel like this and I know I am not alone. It is okay to feel like this; maybe it is even a good thing that I feel like this. It is merely an outward manifestation of my concern for human life – both those I know and those I do not. With the anxiety symptoms I feel physically, running alongside our thoughts – some voluntary, some involuntary, coming from nowhere, out of the blue, unexpected and unwelcome. Nothing positive at all. Not a single thought is positive, not even vaguely. I know what I must do in theory now to manage this anxiety but it's not that easy.

One must try not just once or twice but repeatedly and never ever give up.

One of the very first things to recognise and realise is that anxiety is in itself a normal human emotion/feeling/sensation. As is happiness, sadness, anger, guilt etc. These emotional states are what make us human; without these varying emotions, we would be no different from a robot. We have happy moments, sad moments and angry moments as well as having anxious moments. These are all (on the whole) part of the routine normal fluctuations in the rollercoaster of life. It is when these things become excessive, extreme, unmanageable, and out of proportion to the current situation that further intervention is required. Otherwise, for most people, a few simple strategies to improve their coping skills in times of surging anxiety will be sufficient. Not everyone will be able to adopt all of these measures but even if one or two of these strategies work for you to manage your anxiety symptoms, it will be better than nothing.

One aspect of anxiety management is to try to figure out what the underlying root cause of your anxiety is. What exactly is bothering you? Are there any themes? Often this is not so easy to identify and there may be many interconnected complex issues that people are struggling to process. Some people may be able to process their thoughts. Others will struggle to do that with or without therapy. If this strategy does not work for you, it's okay, don't worry; simply move on to trial the next strategy. Don't get anxious about it! So, in the current crisis as an example, we can easily pin down our anxiety as being as a result of COVID-19 and the fear of losing someone we love. No doubt this is a huge source of worry for many at the moment, but it is proportionate as the threat of life is very real. Perhaps it would be more concerning if we were not anxious about it? So, in this way, we have processed our anxiety and labelled the root cause. The next thing would be to try to think about what brings on the anxiety symptoms. From being relatively relaxed to suddenly feeling a build-up of tension and overwhelming surge of anxiety. Sometimes it is clear what has brought on this change. Other times it is not clear. It is helpful to at least try to identify possible triggers, but it is not always possible. Triggers may be conscious or subconscious, they may be obvious, and they may be hidden. First try to think of any obvious triggers that you are consciously aware of; for example, in the current situation an obvious trigger may be when we hear the latest number of cases or deaths when we read the news/social media. Another obvious trigger is when the thought of losing our loved one comes in our mind. Once we can identify the triggers, we can then move on to try to avoid them or minimise them. If we find that exposure to COVID-19 news or media is triggering our anxiety, what we must do is limit our exposure and try to only view reliable content from reliable sources. We should aim to only expose ourselves to the facts and avoid hearing the debates and opinions of others. These are never-ending and limitless. No doubt everyone is entitled to an opinion and to voice their opinion, but if hearing it is detrimental to your mental health and has a negative effect on you personally, then simply stick to facts. Even just hearing the facts will be anxiety provoking; prepare yourself for that! Cut out all the extras and beware of fake news and conspiracy theories. If you are exposed to it, push it to one side in your mind. Do not allow your mind to start creating its own ideas and web. Take control of your mind and do not be influenced by the false propaganda. Try to only expose yourself to the bare minimum that you need to remain informed. Do not get sucked into the COVID-19 web of information. You do not need to know it all. You still have a life to get on with. To curb the anxieties, limit yourself to how long you will listen to the news and how many times a day. Plan to only watch the main daily press briefings. Put your phone aside if you need to so you can have a mental break from COVID-19. It has already taken over the world; protect your mind from it! Don't forget that anxiety is also highly contagious! When we are worried, stressed and anxious, our minds start working in unhelpful ways. It leads us into traps which we easily fall into. We need to learn about these traps so that we can pick up when it is happening. Recognise any of these patterns of thinking so that you can stop yourself. Take a step back and reassess the situation. Don't trust everything your mind tells you!

One of the commonest mind traps is the tendency of the mind (when faced with a challenge) to automatically leap to the worst-case scenario. This is entirely a normal mode of operating and how our minds are pre-wired. However, it is not always helpful, and for some it is detrimental as they enter a vicious cycle of negative thoughts/images which further elevate their anxieties, leading to more catastrophic thought patterns. It is extremely difficult to get out of these vicious cycles that our mind pulls us into unconsciously and unwillingly. What we can do and should try to do is realise this mind trap and recognise when it happens so that we can prevent ourselves from entering the cycle. We must challenge these thoughts; are they truly accurate? What is the likelihood of the worst-case scenario actually happening? Pretty low actually. Reframe your thoughts; train your mind to think of the positives. For example, the mind will jump to think that your loved one will die from COVID-19, but realistically, there is more chance of survival…as long as we all take the necessary precautions. Anxiety is important; it has a vital role to play in our survival. Extremely unpleasant, no doubt about that, but without it we would not change our ways, we would not take precautions. Anxiety symptoms are our bodies' ways of informing us that we are in danger. This is why it is normal and natural. We should not fear it as it will not harm us. Accept it. What we need to do is respond to our anxieties by taking action, preparing ourselves and taking precautions. Once we have done this, only then will the anxiety begin to decrease. Though it will not disappear entirely, not in the current crisis, and that is fine. We can live with some level of anxiety. If nothing, it will keep us on high alert.

Another mind trap we need to avoid falling into is that of magnifying the negative things and minimising positive things. We must try to do the opposite in our minds to keep objective, realistic and sane in devastating times. Keep your own vision clear. The media will of course focus more heavily on the negatives now. Do not forget the positive things. Try to focus more on the positive side of things. It is not all doom and gloom. Millions upon millions of people are surviving COVID-19, even the elderly; there are reports of people aged over 90 years old surviving too so there is hope. We must not lose hope at this time. Hope will keep us going and will get us out of the other end of this tunnel. Hope that we will soon be safely reunited with our loved ones wherever they may be in the world. Hope that we will once again be in the midst of the hustle and bustle and chaos of everyday life. Hope that we will be surrounded by people in shops, parks, trains, airports etc. The current situation is only temporary and our hopes for a better future will make it bearable and will push us up to make it happen. Even just imagining in your mind's eye the image of what you hope for can provide a moment of peace, a moment of brightness in the darkness we are in. So, as they say, 'hope for the best but prepare for the worst'.

The use of mental imagery or visualisation should be encouraged. Just as the mind can play tricks on us, we too can play tricks on our mind! The subconscious mind cannot tell the difference between a real image or an imagined image, so any image that we imagine has an impact on our subconscious mind. By image, I mean any picture, scene, event, incident that plays out in our mind. Sometimes voluntarily and consciously we imagine it like a daydream, and sometimes it is involuntary. Our mind is constantly constructing imagery either consciously or unconsciously and these are affecting us in more ways than we realise. If we repeatedly visualise negative images/situations/problems, our mindset will be negative and we will bring ourselves down, and this will not help to strengthen our psychological immunity. We must control which mental images we are allowing to enter our subconscious minds. Reject the negative ones and embrace the positive.

You will very soon feel uplifted from within!

Day 10 – 26 March 2020

As of today, a quarter of the entire world is under some sort of lockdown to try to limit the spread of this virus. The UK now has almost 10,000 cases...let's see what today's numbers will be like. We are treading the same path as many other countries. The trajectories are the same; will the death rates be the same too? Harrowing thoughts and images come to mind…

Today I reflect on the concept of 'immunity'. Another buzzword nowadays. Everyone is talking about the concept of herd immunity; some are worried about having low immunity and therefore being at higher risk of a more severe infection. No one is talking about psychological immunity. We need to work on boosting this; it will not happen by itself so we must make the effort to improve our psychological immunity levels. The time is now so that we are in a much better position to cope with the upcoming slaughter and bloodbath. Prepare yourselves. I start by reflecting back on the past week or so. The first week of my entries all seem so negative, desperate and dare I say panicky. A few days ago, I realised this, acknowledged that I was getting trapped in the world of COVID-19 negativity, dread and despair. Like many other people are now. Probably most. I recognise that this is a normal response, but I also recognise that this is not helpful if sustained over a long period of time. This is why I have now adopted a different mindset. One of problem solving, strategic planning, hope and positivity. Not just for the practical stuff in life like how to get groceries, how to keep kids busy at home etc. But also for our mental health, or 'psychological health' would be a more positive term to use. The word 'mental' still has so much negativity connected to it so perhaps we would feel better saying that we need to work on our 'psychological health'. Perhaps this is also a fundamental change needed in our own thinking.

We all know the basics of what we should be doing to look after ourselves. For example, improve sleep, eat healthy, exercise regularly etc. But now more than ever before, we all need more intensive support. Simply improving the above few basic things is not enough. It is wildly insufficient in the current crisis. We may already feel that we are in crisis mode, and we can't manage to focus and work on improving our psychological health now – we have so many other things to do! Believe me, we are only at the base of this cold, daunting iceberg. We are perhaps only at the 10 second point in this one hour if you compare the timescales of where we are in this pandemic with the clock. As we progress further, we will need to increasingly draw on our psychological reserves to get through it. We will find that we have backup reserves that we do not even know of. It is in times of crisis when we are really pushed our limits that we truly become aware of how much we can handle. For now, work on boosting your backup reserves!

So, what more can we do to boost our psychological immunity? There are so many small techniques we can start working on. Of course, we can't do it all in one go but if we promise ourselves to try even one or two every day, it will be better than doing nothing at all. We have already talked about a few tips to manage anxiety, taking control, the power of mental imagery, positivity and hope, social support and forgiveness. Now we should talk about a few more. Whichever concepts/tips/techniques make sense to you, whichever ones you click with, embrace it and adopt it into your daily life, your approach to everything you do. You will soon notice a shift, and a positive shift, in not just your mind but also your feelings and emotions, and even your relationships with others will improve.

We have all heard of the concepts of grounding/meditation/mindfulness and deep breathing exercises. Many of us are so fed up with hearing about these! It often feels so difficult and complicated that we don't even try it. We all know the theory behind it and most of us think that when we are in psychological distress or crisis, we will then think about using these techniques. This however is not the best approach. We cannot expect ourselves to pick up and develop new skills while in the middle of a crisis. These are skills like any other. For example, learning to drive, learning to play an instrument. Don't we learn to drive in quiet empty car parks or learn to play an instrument in a quiet room alone before we drive the car in busy traffic or play the instrument in front of a large audience? Similarly, psychological techniques must be learned and practised in moments of calm so that they can be implemented in moments of psychological chaos. Of course, you probably might not feel the benefits straight away, but rest assured, keep up the practice along the bumpy road and you will get benefit from it.

There are so many techniques that can be tried and so much information about mindfulness. In fact, it is a whole textbook of information and advice. What I will try to do is summarise it concisely and try to explain it clearly so that everyone will find it easy to adopt and follow. We do not have time now to go into and try to understand all the theory behind it all, so essentially this is a shortcut version, like a super-intensive crash course of how to boost psychological immunity. When you know crisis is sadly fast approaching, it's easy to get bogged down in the details in the terminologies etc, but this is not needed. All we need is a simple, clear guide that has been tried and tested, effective and proven to work. We don't all need to examine, dissect and understand the scientific evidence. Just trust an expert in the field!

Mindfulness is basically about training yourself to live in the present moment, to be alert and fully aware of what is happening in the 'here and now'. Not just what is happening in terms of activities but your senses (what you can see/ hear/smell/touch/ taste) as well as your emotions. Life is very busy, and we are all so occupied with various activities, commitments etc. We are constantly multi-tasking and juggling our activities/jobs. How often do we stop everything and take a moment to pause? Not often, not regularly. Are we really that busy that we cannot pause for just a moment? Not even a minute? All it takes is a moment!

As well as practical busyness with daily activities, don't forget that internally we are all very busy too. Our minds, consciously and subconsciously, are active and frantically working your way! Even those people who do not appear busy externally are in their minds internally very active. What we need to do is apply the concepts of mindfulness to our daily routines. It should be incorporated into our way of life. It is an attitude, an approach that is deeply satisfying, nourishing and soothing. The more we adopt these strategies, the more benefit we will see in our lives, in how we feel and how we cope with situations. In some ways, it works in a dose-dependent way – the higher the dose, the stronger its effects will be. Think of it as a simple, easy way to quieten our chattering mind and reduce the background noise. It may be helpful to think of it as switching the channel on your mind's television. Although it sounds complex and difficult to do, any activity, for example, walking, driving, eating, washing dishes, bathing, can be done in a mindful manner. All this means is to be fully aware and fully engaged in that activity. What normally happens is our mind wanders and we get on with things as though we are on autopilot mode.

What we need to do is train ourselves to slow down, focus on what we are doing and allow our mind to be fully present. Find a quiet moment to just sit still comfortably. Imagine your chattering mind as an hourglass timer full of millions of grains of sand, each one resembling a thought/feeling/sensation. Decide to focus on one single grain of sand, perhaps a sound, perhaps the sensation of breathing, perhaps even how your feet feel on the ground. Any one single thing. Just think of that one thing and visualise all the other grains of sand passing down through the narrow space into the other side. Naturally your mind will repeatedly wander and that is okay. Your job is to notice this happening and redirect your mind gently back to that one single thing you are focusing on. The aim is not to force your mind to be silent; this would be an unrealistic and unreasonable expectation. The aim is to train yourself to focus on a single thing. After several attempts to bring your mind back to that one sensation you chose, you will feel the lightness of having a single grain of sand in the top of your hourglass. Allow this to also fall through the hourglass and direct your thoughts to your own body.

Start from your feet and notice the very subtle sensations of tingling/itching/movement etc. Observe the texture of your clothing against your skin. Focus, observe, feel and let the sensation pass. Move your focus up through your legs into your abdomen, feel any tummy grumbles, observe any movement of breathing of your tummy and chest. As you travel up your own body, focus on your breathing. Truly absorb each breath, feel the air travel up and down, in and out of your chest. Continue to feel relaxed, mindful and grounded in the present moment. Once you are ready to resume your other activities, broaden your awareness; gradually allow yourself to notice the sights and sounds around you. As though you have flipped the hourglass again and your mind will be filled to be mindFULL. The brief break you gave your mind will work wonders for you.

Another helpful and potent technique which can be used alongside mindfulness as well as on its own is that of deep breathing exercises. This may sound straightforward but to have its maximum beneficial effect, this too needs to be done using some specific techniques. Once again, there are many deep breathing techniques including counting the number of seconds breathing in and out. I will describe a tried and tested strategy proven to work every time. Some people find it helpful to focus on counting the number of seconds they breathe in and out; others find it distracting. You have to find what works for you. My personal favourite technique of deep breathing does not involve any counting at all. Instead, it involves combining the benefits of deep breathing with visual imagery and audio sensory experiences. Try it; you will not be disappointed. Imagine your breaths as the incoming tidal waves which begin slow and gentle, build in pressure and intensity…crash against the shore and then subside. Imagine seeing these waves and hearing the ocean sounds as you breathe. Steadily breathe in through your nose as much as you possibly can until you feel your tummy inflate like a balloon. Then just when you reach the point where you feel you can't breathe any deeper, take one more attempt to breathe a bit deeper into your reserves... Hold that breathe right there at maximum pressure for a short time... Brace yourself for the incoming tidal auditory crash... Force yourself to exhale through your mouth. The sound will resemble tidal waves crashing against the shore. Repeat this way of breathing for as many repetitions as needed until you feel relaxed. It may also help to visualise the waves washing away your worries, taking them away.

Or even your tensions crashing on the shore and dispersing into nothing...

Day 11 – 27 March 2020

Today there has been one breaking news after another. Just as we digest and absorb one news story, we hear another one. Firstly at 6 a.m., we woke to the news that more than half a million people have tested positive for COVID-19 across the world. All we can do is pray that this number does not reach the next milestone of 1 million. So much bad news already and the day has only just begun. We pray that the rest of the day passes smoothly.

By 9 a.m. we hear tragic news that the first doctor in the UK has died from COVID-19 (RIP). It feels so much closer to home now and a reality. It could be any one of us next. The virus is grimly galloping through the population. All we can do is continue to bubble wrap our homes as much as possible. By midday, news broke that our prime minister is unwell and has tested positive for COVID-19. By 1 p.m., there's news that our health secretary has also tested positive. By the evening news, we hear that our chief medical officer is having COVID-19 symptoms. Can we bear any more bad news in one day? Maybe we should start preparing ourselves for anything and everything…

The sense of uncertainty about the future is leading to fear. Another most unpleasant emotion. Not just uncertainty about the distant future but also of the upcoming imminent future. We have no idea what else we need to face, swallow and digest today. Things are moving at an ever-rapid pace and we are struggling to keep up. There is so much on the line, so much to lose. Each one of us is in mortal danger, there is a grave threat to life, and we have absolutely no idea which of us will be fortunate enough to see the other side of the mountain. Understandably, this causes feelings of fear, and this is entirely normal, but the mind starts racing with negative thoughts and the internal fireworks begin. It is in times like this that we must not isolate ourselves and retreat into our minds, into our own world. There is no benefit to this even though this is what we may feel like doing. This harms us and our loved ones, so please stay connected! Of course, we cannot and should not ignore or downplay our emotions. One helpful strategy is to allocate a set time; a 'worry time', perhaps an hour long, maybe slightly longer if needed, but it definitely should not take over your day! During this time allow your mind to wander, give yourself permission to cry, spend the time focusing on your worries. This is important too. No one is saying don't worry! Once this allocated time is over, you must try to focus on other things. No doubt your mind will every now and then wander back to worry. Notice this happening and tell yourself this is not 'worry time' and set those thoughts aside to be focused on during the next 'worry time' slot.

Outside of the 'worry time' slots, try to revisit things that give you peace and joy. Engage yourself in activities to distract yourself. Keep active physically and psychologically. Do not allow your mind to become a vacuum, as only negative thoughts will expand to fill the vacuum. Be aware of this happening! Don't be hard on yourself; be aware of your self-talk. Be kind to yourself and allow yourself to feel the rollercoaster of emotions. You may be surprised at how you are managing or feeling nowadays. Be patient. You will feel back to your normal self soon. Until then, bear with it and try to find the joy in small things and have a laugh. Do things that elevate your mood. This will vary from person to person: some find joy in cooking, reading and playing sports. Others enjoy watching movies or talking to their loved ones. Sometimes it is even difficult to find joy in things we used to enjoy, and this is normal too. One strategy is to find something that gives you a sense of purpose, a feeling of achievement. We all need to feel that we are doing something useful, something to be proud of. A sense of accomplishment is a huge positive boost to our feeling of personal worth. Some people might learn a new skill: singing, playing an instrument, learning a new language, drawing, writing stories, decorating, handicraft and sewing. Creative activities are particularly good at boosting mood and positivity. The sense of pride you feel and the feeling of satisfaction and accomplishment you will experience when you make something with your own bare hands using your own ideas is surreal. Nothing else can match this feeling, and the feelings and sentiments remain long after you have completed the project. In future, whenever you feel down and sad, simply looking at your project will help you feel better. It will bring back positive feelings of hope. It may even be a helpful reminder of how you feel on a good day. Like memories of the day you finally completed the project, you will get that warm fuzzy feeling inside again and again. If you make something with your own hands for someone you love, they too will benefit from it. Every time they look at it. They will see far more than what you made. They will see and feel your love for them, and there's no greater feeling in the world than love!

For those we truly and wholeheartedly love... Why do we love them? What is it about them that we love? How can we even begin to imagine a life without them? Why do our heart/soul feel so intertwined, connected and super-glued to them? In true unconditional love, thinking of the answer to these questions is mind-boggling and leaves a vacant space in our minds. This is because true love resides in our heart/soul and matters of the heart/soul have nothing to do with the mind. That is the reason why these questions will always remain unanswered. There are no words. If you have an answer/explanation to these questions, then it is not true unconditional love. Of course, that does not mean that you do not love them; there are many different types of love, after all... It is just a different type. What I'm talking about is something else...

True love has no explanations, but it has all the answers. True love is limitless and has no boundaries, yet it is often restrained by the mind. True love expects nothing, and it accepts all. It is ever-understanding, ever-forgiving, ever-lasting. It never dies. It never diminishes. It is like a slow, deeply burning fire which will quietly simmer in the background forever. Even after one partner sadly dies (physically), true love will remain. That feeling will never die. It is the feeling of true love that gives us courage, peace, joy, satisfaction and happiness. The list of positive effects is endless; same as true love itself. True love is the highest and most superior of all human emotions. It secures us, protects us... We have the power to protect each other. We are each other's padlock, and we hold each other's keys. Only with our true love can we be opened up, comfortable and vulnerable. There is an absence of fear in true love, which has the power to heal us. Like parts of a puzzle coming together, true love completes us. The other half of our heart/soul is our missing piece and once we find this, it completes our treasure. With our true love, we naturally fit; everything easily clicks and falls into place. We feel like we are one heart, one soul, split between two physical bodies...and it is this distance between us physically that stretches the two halves of the one heart/soul. But like an elastic band, however much it is stretched, it will always recoil back to its core centre. So, in this way, two halves of one heart/soul will always be together and reunited. Even if one half physically is no more, his or her love will recoil back to the other remaining half. In this way, true love never dies. True love is in itself energizing, refreshing and motivating. It requires no effort at all; it happens all by itself. We do not need to even try to understand each other. We know, understand and accept our true love instinctively and intuitively. We are one and the same heart and soul, after all.

We hurt together, we cry together, and our hearts always sing together... Melodious and free, like true love should always be!

Day 12 – 28 March 2020

Every night we sleep in fear of what we have to face the next day…and every morning we wake in fear of what we have missed while we were sleeping. For a split second, upon waking, we are not aware that we are still living in the middle of coronavirus times. This does not last long, however, and even before we have fully opened our eyes, we feel compelled to reach out to our phone/device. We cannot resist this; we feel the need to be informed of the latest developments across the world. We are not expecting good news, but even then, we struggle to keep away. After all, now our devices are our connection to the outside world. Until now, by morning in the past few weeks since we entered coronavirus times, our devices have been bombarded with coronavirus related news/information/advice. All being sent by people all across the world, in various times zones, so it is as though we are connected to 24 hours' slow drip-feed of coronavirus talk. This is what is now nourishing us. We struggle to switch off from it all, but the importance of switching off and taking regular short breaks from coronavirus times cannot be overemphasised. We must regularly throughout the day, multiple times, set ourselves free and enjoy some 'coronavirus-free time'. This means we switch off any route by which virus-related stuff can reach us. We must even agree with each other that we will not discuss anything related to the virus. Use this time slot to distract yourself, have a laugh, reminisce fond old memories, revitalise and renourish your heart, mind and soul…so that you can return to coronavirus times and face the next upcoming challenges in a better way. Use these 'coronavirus-free time' slots wisely. Really value these and view these as an escape from reality. A time for some much needed 'me time', not just that but 'us time'. We must not ignore our loved ones; they need us to pull them up, and if this seems too difficult, we must simply hold hands to stop each other from falling any further.

Just as no five fingers are the same, the same is true of our loved ones. Each and every one of us has a unique style, our own way of approaching and understanding things, and of course every one of us manages and copes with things in our own individually unique way. We need to try to understand our loved ones better, put ourselves in their shoes and try to see things from their eyes. Even within the same family, living in the same house, we will all be standing at different windows and looking at the same scenario. We need to develop an empathy towards our loved ones; we must respond to them and not react to them. Easily said, I know, but we must try. When we react (and we often do this immediately), we are actually increasing the divide between us. We should take a deep breath to carefully recalibrate our thoughts and emotions before we reply and engage in conversations. Words once said, especially in the heat of the moment, resonate deeply in our loved ones and the ripples may go on forever. Therefore, it is vital we speak kindly, lovingly and respectfully. Always speak softly and be aware of your tone and style. Recalibrate yourself regularly and find other ways to release your frustrations. Taking it out on your nearest and dearest may feel like the easiest thing to do – after all, they are an easy target – but do not take them for granted. They too have feelings. Whenever you open your mouth to speak, make sure scented flower petals come out instead of scorching fireballs. If you can't produce flower petals, keep quiet until you can. Protect your loved ones from your own fireballs...and don't forget that prolonged repeated injuries take longer to heal and are also more difficult to treat. Just think of the same bone being repeatedly broken…in the same way, emotional pains are no different. On the face of it, our nearest and dearest may look perfectly fine and calm, but can you know for sure what is going on inside? Can you say for certain how much salt or sugar is dissolved in a liquid (tea, coffee or juice) just by looking at it?

Just think that the person in front of you may be using all of their psychological reserves just to be able to master the courage to face others. They may be using all of their psychological energy to keep themselves composed just so that they can present themselves in front of you. This is why kindness is so very important. Make it one of your core principles in life. Always be kind to everyone; young and old, those you know and those you do not, those who are obviously unwell and those who appear well. Don't ever be the reason for someone else's pain, be it physical or emotional. Don't ever pick on other people's wounds, be that physical or emotional. Kindness goes a long way. One way of understanding this further is to think of gardening. Plants need daily tender loving care (TLC), watering and sunlight. This is their nourishment, and in the same way, our personal relationships need daily TLC, watering and showering with kindness and love. Only then will our relationships blossom. Without this they too will wither away. We must make sure we water the roots of our relationships, not just the more superficial branches. For some people this seems an alien concept; some are so engrossed in themselves and their own affairs to even think of their loved ones in such a way, let alone think of others like this. It is all too easy to take others for granted. It doesn't always come naturally to everyone either. Some people are naturally kind, others need to work on it. We should all make a real conscious effort to improve the quality of our relationships with others. The first step towards this would be to improve our vision so we can more easily understand things from another person's perspective. We all sit on different panes of glass of a diamond prism and look at the same scenario from slightly different angles. Or think of it as we are all travelling on the same aeroplane, and we all have a different view of what is outside the window. Just as we cannot see clearly in the dark or if we are wearing blindfolds or sunglasses; in the same way, we cannot see our loved ones clearly. Remove the blindfold of negativity, put aside the tinted glasses of ego and shine the light to brighten up your life and relationships. Remove the blinkers and open your eyes; open the gates of your heart and mind.

Day 13 – 29 March 2020

Yesterday we slept after hearing the following:

- The UK has now has more than 1000 deaths

- Italy now has more than 10,000 deaths

- The world now has more than 600,000 cases

How can anyone sleep in peace after hearing this? There was so much excitement about the year 2020 when we were safely back in 2019, so much eager anticipation that 2020 only comes once in a generation and so we should plan some sort of memorable event. We have definitely got this, and whenever we hear the word 2020, we will automatically feel shivers and chills. A haunting cursed year full of doom and gloom, uncertainty and fear, chaos and crisis. Is this all that 2020 will be remembered for? Do we really want this to be imprinted on our hearts and minds forever? Is there any silver lining on cloud 2020 at all? Of course, there is…there are always two sides to every coin. Now is the time to flip the coin and view the other side.

In the hustle and bustle, chaos and competition of modern-day life, perhaps we have begun to lose sight of the core values and principles. Are we not all so excessively over-stretched like an elastic band ready to snap at any time? Do we not all struggle to squeeze time and energy to fulfil the needs of those we love? What about having the time and energy to fill our own personal needs? Do we not continue with our hectic lives just fulfilling our commitments like tick box exercises? Do we feel that our loved ones don't notice us doing this? Have they too become a tick box exercise? Do we treat ourselves as a tick box exercise? When was the last time we truly connected, engaged with and fulfilled our loved ones' needs? Or were we always too busy? How many times has someone we loved needed us, but we could not be there for them? Is this how life should be? Is this how we want our lives to be? The other side of the coin is of reflection, re-evaluation, recalibration, rejuvenation and re-setting (5 Rs). When we cannot change the situation as it is out of our hands (like the coronavirus crisis), we must take control of our mindset and adjust our focus, edit our approach to the situation. That is to say flip the coin today!

COVID-19 has frozen the world in terrible fear. For some the 'pause' button has been pressed and for others unfortunately the 'stop' button will be pressed. No one knows whether they are in the life 'paused' or life 'stopped' group. For now, we can only hope that our life has been simply put on hold, on 'pause'. We must use this 'pause' time wisely; we must respect it and value it. There is a deep-seated purpose behind this pause: the 5 Rs.

To be able to reflect effectively and efficiently, we must first understand what it means to reflect. The simplest and most basic analogy would be to look at yourself in the mirror. Some people might find it easier to think of it as looking at themselves in a body of lake water and seeing their reflection. Give yourself time (free from distraction) to just sit and think. Let your mind run free. Dig deep inside yourself and contemplate. Review your life experiences, feelings and emotions. Rewind and remind yourself of decisions you have made. How have you chosen to live your life? Ask yourself what? Why? How? Examine and analyse your attitudes, approach, actions and behaviour. Probe yourself deeper than you normally do. This will help gain perspective so we can decide how we want to proceed with the rest of our lives. No one is perfect, we are all using trial and error and we are all continuously learning and developing. By reflecting regularly, we can truly grow. There is no time like the present for us to honestly reflect on ourselves. In moments of uncertainty and crisis, perhaps it is easier to gain clarity and perspective. We hope that positivity and personal growth will come out of the current COVID-19 crisis.

If something is not working as best as we would like; or could be done better, we must demonstrate flexibility and a willingness to adjust ourselves. Take a step back, distance yourself from yourself, see yourself from the outside, as an outsider, almost like watching yourself and your life on a cinema screen. Sit back and enjoy the show! You will probably find that how easily you have got stuck in a routine confined by the constraints of your culture, boundary by the invisible rules of your comfort zone. Now is the time to re-evaluate and recalibrate ourselves so that when we emerge on the other side of the coronavirus mountain, we will be a new and improved version of ourselves. If we all do this, the post-COVID-19 world will be a better place.

No doubt It will once again be busy, and we will all be submerged in our commitments and daily grind. Really though, it's all about priorities at the end of the day, isn't it? We all know deep in our heart of hearts that we will find the time from somewhere for the things we really sincerely want to do, and if we don't genuinely want to, we have all the excuses under the sun at our fingertips!

A few questions to reflect on:

- Am I living the best life I possibly can?
- Am I using my time effectively and productively or am I wasting valuable time?
- Am I living each day as though it could be my last?
- Who matters the most/who I can't live without?
- Who do I love and who will I miss?
- Who loves me and who will miss me?
- How do I want people to remember me once I am gone/what is my legacy?

Day 14 – 30 March 2020

The numbers continue to thunder past us daily, leaving us in a terrible turmoil. We are having to cope and adjust to the situation at an ever-alarming rate. Things we had never even thought of as possibilities in this day and age. We lived in times of freedom, independence, comfort and fortunately safety and good health. Now it feels as though all of this is on the line and the stakes are higher than we imagine; higher than what is being predicted, perhaps.

Those who are fortunate enough to be spending their days of isolation and social distancing in busy households are blessed beyond measure. They have plenty of company, time to spend with their families, sufficient business, to pass the time. In fact, some households may now be over busy, close to absolute mayhem at times! Parents working from home, children playing and studying at home, no outings, no shopping trips, nothing. Isn't this perfect in some ways? Doing everything together all the time? This enforced and locked-up downtime may be great for some; perfect for those who love to stick together with their families. Each household is now no different than a deserted Island…and who would you want to be stranded on a desert island with? Hopefully those people are already with you. On your island, if not, thank God for technology! Use it to bring those from other islands into yours. Share your space, share your activities, share your love! Physical distance should not come between us, and we must use technologies like video calls to bridge these distances and close any gaps…before it is too late. Then there will only be regrets. Each individual island is now a risk to others but only a physical risk. We must welcome others to enter our islands (via technology) in a warm, emotional embrace. Hug those you love with your words, emotions and sentiments. Until the days when normality returns…

Spare a thought for those who may be less fortunate. Those who live alone, those who have no friends or family, those who cannot afford food let alone the latest technologies to survive this gloomy phase of lonely existence. Those living in the hustle and bustle of their own households imagine what it must be like to be all alone at home. For many people, this is a reality not just in coronavirus times but all the time. Now with the universal, national lockdown, an eerie silence is spreading and has reached us. The usual sound of people, music, cars is no more. Only silence remains outside, not to mention stillness. There is nothing to see from the window, no movement, no other human; where is everybody? All hiding inside. Some islands are busier than others; some are painfully quiet, but does silence itself have a sound? It is in moments of silence and stillness that our thoughts are amplified. Some are positive, some are negative, some voluntary, some intrusive and unwanted, some are soothing, and some are terrifying. How can someone escape from their own thoughts especially if living alone with no distractions? Spare a thought for such people.

Thoughts will come and thoughts will go; some will be brief visitors just passing by, while others will no doubt overstay their welcome. If only we could control them, like so many other things in these times, but they are not in our hands. Some are constant like the screensaver or display picture of our mind and some pop up out of nowhere, often at the most unexpected times, throwing us completely off guard. If only we only ever had good, pleasurable and positive thoughts. What should we do about the horrible negative thoughts, which for many nowadays are about the coronavirus, thoughts of death, thoughts of living but without our loved ones. Perhaps we need to accept that negative thoughts can be normal too. Perhaps we should accept that just as we cannot control the coronavirus, we cannot also control all of our thoughts. Of course, we can try, but no doubt some will get through the filters and barriers we set up in our mind. Perhaps we do not need to understand it all. Perhaps what we should do is work on identifying and labelling these thoughts. Be more aware of our thoughts and the impact they have on your feelings and behaviours.

Ideally, we should ensure that the main themes of the backdrop of our mind is a positive one. Allow the pop-ups to occur; don't try to fight them. Just leave them in the background. The more you focus on the negative thoughts, the stronger they will become. Try to minimise the importance you give them. Choose which thoughts you give value and time to. Make positivity your aim and hope for a better life once through this dark tunnel of COVID-19. For now, we must ride it through to the other side. Spare a thought for those who are isolated all alone at home with nothing but their own thoughts for company. Reach out to them, speak with them; perhaps you could be the only person they speak to that day. You too will benefit from this. The peace and joy we get from giving to and helping others is immensely greater than what we get from taking and helping ourselves.

Day 15 – 31 March 2020

Let's be grateful, thankful and appreciative of what we have. However little or however much we have. Whatever we have is enough for us and in it, we will find peace, joy and happiness. Whether we are stranded on a deserted island with many people or if we are stranded on a deserted island with few people or completely alone. We can all find something to be thankful for and we should strive to be more appreciative overall. We might automatically think of the bigger obvious things in life for which we are very thankful, but don't forget the smaller things, the things we take for granted daily. If you are able to see clearly, hear easily, walk and move your body without pain or difficulty, you already have so much to be grateful for. So many across the world are struggling to breathe because of COVID-19. Should we not be thankful that we can still take deep breaths easily? There is plenty for us to be grateful for if only we open our minds and adopt an attitude of thanks. Today's figures were announced as 25,150 cases and 1789 deaths in the UK alone. We must express our gratitude to have a life itself. Thankfully, we are safe and well and not amongst the 842,811 people affected or 41,429 dead across the world. They too had hopes and plans for the future, but it's now too late for them. Maybe it's not too late for us to reach out to others, be grateful and enjoy our precious time together in this world.

Those of us who are blessed to have children will no doubt be extremely grateful to have them. After all, nothing can compare to the joy that children bring, but times like the present make us wonder and worry about our children. Their future, their social, emotional, psychological development as well as their memories of these times. We live in an immensely competitive world. We all know that everyone is driving to be at the top in all walks of life. What the coronavirus crisis has taught us is that we all are fundamentally equal at the basic level. Our fundamental feelings, requirements and necessities are actually very similar regardless of status, race, religion etc.

The COVID-19 competition is one where everyone wants to be at the bottom!

Day 16 – 1 April 2020

Traditionally, 1 April marks a significant point in the UK calendar. The clocks have sprung forwards, the days will now be longer, and the weather warms up. We are now officially in British Summer Time and spring is finally here. We wait all winter for this day, we even celebrate it with April Fool's Day and have a laugh. 1 April 2020, no one is laughing. Everyone is serious, everyone is busy processing, digesting and absorbing. Some were completely consumed and overwhelmed. At times like this, it is important to keep tight hold of the things that make us smile, laugh and have fun. We should continue to chit-chat, make each other laugh and tease each other in positive ways. Having a laugh with someone we love will very easily wash away our worries and break down our burdens. We could even play games, activities and remind us of ourselves of the pre-COVID-19 era. What did life it was? What do we now miss the most about it? What will change about it? How will we live better in the post-COVID-19 era?

Today marks a new beginning: a new month, but it will most probably be a worse month than the one we have just passed, coped with, adjusted to and most importantly survived. We know deep inside ourselves and regardless of how positive we are trying to be that the fact and reality of 2020 so far is nothing short of a real-life sci-fi horror movie. We have all been transported to a parallel universe in the most gripping movie ever. Alongside everything else that has changed recently, even our sense of time is no longer the same. Even this time last month, time was flying past; we were racing in fifth gear, and we were only wishing that we could bump up to sixth, seventh, eighth, nineth, tenth gear somehow. We were running on empty fuel tanks yet expecting so much from ourselves. We had depleted our psychological reserves and our backup supplies; but despite this, we continued running on the hamster wheel of life. All without pausing, without taking much-needed, well-deserved breaks. We ignored ourselves and our loved ones in some ways. Now the whole world is taking a break…

The past few weeks, time has passed so slowly, painfully slowly. Each day has felt like a month in itself. Perhaps this is because we have been forced to slow down; perhaps we are less busy; perhaps we do not know what to do with ourselves. Have we forgotten how to enjoy our own company and just be with our self? There is no doubt that our sense of time is related to our mindset; when we are in a good place psychologically speaking, time does not bother us. We are even blissfully unaware of it. Yet when we are in a bad psychological space, time itself becomes painful; an awful sensation that we feel above and beyond all of our other senses.

With the start of a new month comes the feeling of refreshment, the start of a new chapter; if only we turn the page. Last month was spent in turmoil, turbulence and terror. It has been a rollercoaster of emotions; not just fast and furious but at times slow, unnerving, anticipatory dread. We can be certain that April will only be worse. Perhaps we will feel like our seat belts/restraints on the rollercoaster have loosened now…

Though we will continue to have no control over so many things which we once did, we will always have control of how we choose to respond. We are in charge of our own personal attitude and approach, even in times of complete chaos and crisis. It is of course all too easy to forget this, and our feelings, thoughts and emotions will very easily cast a shadow and blur our vision. We must be aware and mindful that this will happen so that we can try to pull ourselves out of this trap. The more we try to do this, the easier it will become.

For now, let's continue to focus our energies on living better in the 'here and now'. The past is most definitely behind us, and the future is yet to come. All that truly and genuinely exists is the present. Tackle things as they come, one day at a time, one hour at a time, sometimes even one minute or second at a time. Live each and every moment, feel and appreciate it, do something useful and memorable, don't let it rush past like so much of the past. Use your time wisely; after all, it is a valuable commodity. If nothing else makes sense, just use your time to help lift someone else. Just be with someone you love.

Day 17 – 2 April 2020

Spring is definitely here! Even just the word 'spring' itself brings with it a feeling of energy, vibrancy and uplifting joy. Released from the gloom of winter, spring is a natural reminder of nature itself. Its beauty, its freshness, its usefulness, its purpose all come to mind. Life in these times has been stripped down to the bare essentials, the bare necessities. No more unnecessary extras, no more fancy showing off, no more racing to out beat others. We have reached the roots of life itself, and now would be a prime time to think about the roots of nature.

Those of us who are fortunate enough to have their own personal and private garden or outdoor space should consider ourselves blessed. Feel for those who are cooped up in small flats with no access to the outdoors during lockdown. We can all open our windows, allow fresh air to filter its way throughout the home. The fresh air will not only cleanse your home, but it will also help refreshen your mood and your mind in general. We can also spend time looking at the sky, either from our gardens, balconies or windows. What is there to look at in the sky, you might wonder? The vast open sky is full of mystery and amazement; each and every cloud you will see will be unique in all ways, shapes, size, colour, density etc. Even the way in which each individual cloud glides across the sky is fascinating. Spend some time daily just gazing at the sky, its contents, its behaviour. Appreciate it and imagine your worries as the clouds drifting away. Clouds will come and clouds will go; some will be pretty, some will be daunting; but whatever they are like, they will continue to come and go. Thoughts, feelings, and worries are all like that too. Allow them to pass freely; don't challenge them, don't fight them. Just maintain your focus on the sky, the overall bigger picture. Don't forget to notice the birds freely roaming the world while you are stuck inside your home, stuck inside your mind. Free yourself from the chains of your own mind. Be like that bird you see!

If the sun has joined you to brighten up your day, welcome and appreciate it. Allow it to flood your home, allow its rays to ripple through your mind. If you can go outdoors, do that; sit, stand or lie down in the sun. If you can't go outdoors, stick your head or your hands out of the window. Really feel the sun roasting your skin, enjoy and embrace its warmth and its natural healing powers. Another aspect of nature which we can all enjoy is the wonder of water. Be it in the form of rainwater or running water from our showers, bath taps or kitchen taps. Running water from any source has magical benefits for our mental health. Even our hosepipe or sprinkles in the garden we must enjoy and utilise effectively. We should connect with water regularly and really feel its cooling properties. Not only does water have the potential to cool our body but it can also cool our overheated mind. Water is a source of nourishment for all life forms, and we are able to use water to nourish plants and flowers in our gardens. If not, we should try to grow an indoor house plant. Watching plants grow gives a sense of purpose, achievement and satisfaction. If we have no other options, we can always play sounds of nature music on our devices and have that as background noise instead of our chattering mind. Involve the various aspects of nature into your daily routine as much as you possibly can. You will benefit and gain some peace in this otherwise upside down, inside out phase of life also known as COVID-19 times. Don't forget that enjoying nature is a multi-sensory experience which will help to ground you in the 'here and now'. Focus on the sights, the sounds, the textures, the smells and even the taste of nature. Don't just eat or drink your meals and snacks; pause and take the time to notice their tastes and textures. Engage all your senses and have a more wholesome dining experience.

So often we eat and drink, but we are not focused on what we are eating/drinking – our mind is elsewhere. This is no truer than at the present moment. Often, we feel so anxious about COVID-19 that we do not feel like eating, and if we do, we are only half eating, as only our body is being nourished. We are not nourishing the mind. Maximise the benefits for your mind by being fully present in the present moment.

Day 18 – 3 April 2020

The nights continue to merge into the days and the living nightmare continues. There are no signs of it abating anytime soon. Weekdays and weekends are all rolled into one. All days feel the same. We have lost an important aspect of our lives: routine. There is much comfort in routine, predictability and timetables. This is ingrained in us from a very early age; from our parents maintaining a family routine when we are of preschool age. Then our schoolteachers followed by college university staff, not to mention the routines we have when we are employed. Now we feel lost. We have lost our routine; it feels like a distant dream. Now is the time to demonstrate our flexibility, our agility, our ability to adjust. We must create a new routine for our lockdown period and until we do, we will continue to feel like we are lost and floundering.

It has now been two weeks since we lived our past life; the longest two weeks ever (for us anyway). The past few days have brought with it a change in tempo, a change in direction of the wind. We have now gotten used to hearing about the coronavirus cases and deaths; that is all we have heard in 2020. Even then, it still felt distant at times, not yet personal. A certain type of news has now begun to seep through; the type we were dreading. In the past few days, we have been hearing of a 'friend of a friend', acquaintances, distant relatives etc who have sadly died from COVID-19. Heart-wrenching and tragic news, each time feeling more and more like a personal attack. At the moment, it feels as though news is seeping through the narrow gap between our front door and the door frame. We fear that news like this will shortly be breaking our door down, overwhelming us with sadness and fear. How can we better prepare ourselves for what is fast approaching? Is it even possible to prepare for something of this magnitude? Surely, this is what the pre-vaccine era must have been like. We are not the first generation to suffer like this, but we sure do hope that we will be the last. We can better appreciate the importance of vaccines, now that we have had personal experience of living in a pre-COVID-19 vaccine era. We have had not just a taste of a pre-vaccine era, but a full blown all you can eat buffet platter!

We can only comfort ourselves and support each other in times like this and words play a vital role in doing this. Either verbal or written words have the power to heal and console in moments of psychological trauma. Each death from COVID-19 we hear about pushes us down further into the deep dark lonely well we are already barely clinging on to. It is only natural that we feel this way and it is extremely difficult, and the pain we feel is beyond measure. Many things in life remain a mystery, are unexplainable and are left unanswered. Accepting or even understanding this is no easy feat and begins to go beyond the realms of the human mind. After all, do we really need to understand it all? Must everything in life be rational, logical or fair? It is undoubtedly extremely difficult to navigate through a pandemic like COVID-19; similarly, navigating through distressing and complex emotions is also a mammoth task. We can only take it one day at a time. No one ever forgets; scars will remain, and we will never be the same again. The world may also never be the same again.

Tears will grow and tears will flow; tears will say all that we do not even know. From our deepest heart of hearts, tears strike us like piercing darts. Tears are a language like no other, expressing emotions we try so hard to smother. That which is hidden so deeply inside, can only come out using tears as their ride. A single teardrop can sweeten the saltiest ocean, silently soothing the inner indescribable commotion. Tears speak the unexplainable, unexpressed turmoil, for they are essentially the true language of the soul. Hidden by the thick curtains of the eyes, true feelings lie on the road behind the eyes. A roadmap unseen by most and travelled by very few, beyond blessed are those who have someone by their side to help them navigate through.

Day 19 – 4 April 2020

The past few weeks have been one big blur; days have merged with no distinction between weekdays and weekends. We are merely rolling from day to night and night to day. There are no breaks, and the rolling continues. Our routines and structures on which we base our daily lives seem a distant past, yet it was only just a few weeks ago that we were all living to a closely kept routine. Now the very foundation of our existence has been shaken, so it is no surprise that anything we build on this also feels 'wobbly'. Did we even realise the importance of our routines, structures and boundaries? Most probably we took so much of it for granted. Even the simple process of changing from our work/school clothes into our home clothes in the evening would send an unconscious signal to our mind that our workday has ended and now it is time to relax. Simple routines can provide huge psychological comfort and can help shift our mindset even without us consciously trying to. Nowadays, it seems we have lost our previous routines and are being forced to either have no routines or to rapidly develop and adapt new routines. Another aspect of adjustment we are struggling with. There are so many struggles now; when will it all end and go back to normal? Will it be a new normal or will we go back to the normal life as we once knew it? Will it be an abnormal normal? Who knows what the future will bring with it? For now, all we can do is try to prepare ourselves for any eventuality. Anything is possible. Make peace with this fact. Accept it as it is. No ifs and buts.

There is one thing that is consistently proving to be an anchor for us: the UK daily government press conference at 5 p.m. on weekdays and 4 p.m. on weekends (the only thing differentiating weekdays from weekends!). We drop everything and watch intently at the latest developments. We even schedule our day around it, look forward to and appreciate it. Without it perhaps, we would feel even more lost, stranded and isolated. Thinking of this reiterates the value of having a routine of predictable schedule, an anchor amidst chaos. A routine provides us with something to focus on and holds even more value in times of stress and uncertainty. Providing a framework, a skeleton upon which we can flesh out our lives. A routine is our anchor amidst the storm, preventing us from straying too far and is grounding in many ways.

Day 20 – 5 April 2020

The past few weeks have been too tumultuous to sum it up in one single word. The initial days were drowned in COVID-19 information, fear, uncertainty and panic. An overall, overarching and overwhelming feeling of dread. This phase brought with it a sense of urgency, a brutal realisation of the need for rapid adjustment. Not only in the practical, physical sense of how we live and manage our daily affairs, but also in the psychological sense. We have had to demonstrate our psychological plasticity and be moulded and re-moulded in a way that has also been unprecedented. In times of crisis, particularly those such as COVID-19 which required tremendous adjustment all under a significant time pressure, our true capabilities and underlying personalities are unveiled. We have had to adapt to the new lifestyle and environment to our self. This has been a dynamic drive through our deepest darkest jungle. Not just in terms of the COVID-19 situation, but our psychological adaptations to it. We have risen to this demanding coronavirus challenge as we have done so previously to many changes in our past, and we have in the past come out of the deepest darkest jungles, re-emerging as new and improved versions of ourselves. Updated versions!

A common cliché we have all heard numerous times before is 'what does not kill you makes you stronger', and it feels truer now in coronavirus times than it has ever done before. We have travelled a million miles at a speed we never imagined or thought possible after a rocky launch into coronavirus times. Fortunately, we had our psychological harnesses firmly attached; at times of course, these got loosened and we were shaken to our very core. Nevertheless, our journey through turmoil tunnel followed by a period of rapid adjustment has brought us to where we now are and where we have been for the past few days, a period of surrender, acceptance and a phase of contentment, peace and satisfaction. Knowing that we are taking control of ourselves, our attitudes and our approach to life in general. We are enjoying spending our days and nights with those we love in the most basic and simplistic way. We never thought simplistically could be so serene. Somewhere along life's journey, we had become lost in a materialistic world, surrounded by superficiality and hounded by artificial mask-like relationships. Now all masks have been removed and genuine, deep and sincere truth prevail. Some of us had even forgotten what the ground feels like. Our feet had left the ground in the hope of catching the most elusive things, in the hope of being able to streamline and separate the tangled web of our numerous variable kites. No doubt kites are designed to soar, and they always will, but we humble humans are not. By nature, we are designed to remain on the ground, earthed by reality and connected by deep underground roots. We are now being forced to dig deep, rebuild and reconnect with our roots. In this lies our solace, satisfaction and salvation.

Perhaps selfishness had taken over and consumed us; perhaps we had forgotten how to be selfless, or perhaps we knew but we didn't have the time or energy to be selfless; after all, the 'soaring' is exhausting both physically and psychologically. With it, COVID-19 has brought along the realisation and awareness that 'no man is an island'; is there any single human who truly has no ties, no links, nothing to do with another living creature? We are all so intricately connected in some way or other.

Some links are stronger and more obvious. Others are weaker, fainter or hidden. Nonetheless, a connection is there. Whether we like it or not and regardless of if we are even aware of it or not. We are all like dominoes; whatever we do or say has a ripple effect. When one stands, we all stand. When one falls, we all fall. If only we had realised and understood this before. It had taken the coronavirus to teach us this; lessons we will surely never forget. After all, now we only focus on our main vital priorities: health, food, relationships.

Everything else is an unnecessary extra luxury; the sprinkles on a cupcake!

Day 21 – 6 April 2020

We have been in a lovely place of just simply being, a peaceful existence of true bliss in the comfort of our own homes surrounded by those we love. Even our stresses and anxieties have disappeared (mostly). The coronavirus news and information no longer surprises, scares or shocks us; even the numbers of new cases don't seem to throw us off our course. We remain firmly standing at the helms of our boat riding through the gigantic waves. We are doing this very well and have come a long way from where we were only just a few weeks ago when we were regularly being thrown overboard, waiting for someone to reach out to us somehow by hand or by throwing us some sort of life ring which we clutched on to tightly to stop ourselves from drowning even further. Now we stand firm and connected; our social chains are tight and harness us from disaster. We are in a good place now. There has been a new regularity, a new routine, almost a new beginning. We are at peace with ourselves, with each other and even with COVID-19. Today we woke to news that once again has thrown us overboard. We learn that our prime minister has been admitted to hospital overnight for further COVID-19-related tests. This news brings with it emotional disruption of uncertainty and fear. We allow ourselves to feel this way; after all, this would be the normal way to respond.

The number of cases diagnosed in the world is now well above 1 million, and what about the number of undiagnosed and untested? The mind boggles and descends into panic mode once again. As we approach the peak, we know that the toughest days are yet to come. The past few days seem to have skipped past us, most likely because our mindset was shifted onto a different wavelength. Our focus was elsewhere, on a much better place. We were using our psychological immunity effectively to protect ourselves. Now it feels that that barrier has weakened. Now 600–700 people are dying in each 24-hour time period, and we know that this number will most likely increase; perhaps even more than 1000 people a day will die when we are at the apex of this gigantic, monstrous mountain called COVID-19. The uphill struggle has been a battle beyond comprehension; each step up has been laborious, but we had no choice but to step up. Like driving a small, old car up a steep hill, we have also dragged up and depleted all of our physical and psychological energies. As we approach the hardest, deepest and deadliest segment of this journey, we also need to give it our hardest, deepest and deadliest response.

We are safe and settled for now, but who knows what tomorrow will bring. There are still so many uncertainties, and we are already running on empty fuel tanks, trying our utmost to refuel ourselves. Now is not the time to weaken our resolve to get through this. Now is the time to really pull out all of the stops to protect ourselves from COVID-19, both physically and psychologically. Easy to say though, isn't it? What can we now do that we have not done so far? How can we now double-wall our psychological defence barriers? As we approach the upcoming peak point of this mountain, it is all too easy to focus on it.

Perhaps we should take a moment to see beyond the peak, the view on the other side. After all, what goes up must come down…

9 781917 293778